The ABZ's of School Law
For
Teachers

Dr. Patricia A. McNames

Ed.D, University of Louisville, 1995
E.D.S., Indiana University, 1985
M.S., Indiana University Southeast, 1978
B.A., University of Kentucky, 1972

The ABZ's of School Law for Teachers

Copyright © 2010

Dr. Patricia A. McNames

ISBN: 978-0-615-36298-4
First Printing: May 2010—2000

Library of Congress Control Number:
2010905168

FOR INFORMATION CONTACT:
Dr. Patricia A. McNames
755 Grand Blvd # 105-309
Miramar Beach, FL 32550
502-548-0195

Please visit our web site at
www.schoollaw101.com
Online ordering is available for products and seminars.

Printed in the USA
Morris Publishing®
3212 E. Hwy. 30 * Kearney, NE 68847
800-650-7888 * www.morrispublishing.com

This book is dedicated to the excellent teachers who served as role models throughout the years and who have impacted my life. Teachers such as Mrs. Hadley, Mrs. Lewis, Mrs. Smith, Mr. Bob, Dr. John Moody, and numerous others were the ones who emulated superb teaching on a daily basis. To my teaching colleagues, not only in the public schools but also in the universities, thank you for imparting your knowledge of pedagogy and guiding me to **always do what is best for kids.**

To my wise mother, Flo McNames, and my loving husband, Larry Kunkel, thank you from the bottom of my heart for being the best teachers and the best friends one could ever have.

Acknowledgements

The writing of this book, <u>The ABZ's of School Law For Teachers,</u> would have been impossible without the help and guidance of many people. I am deeply indebted to the following people for their assistance and encouragement during the two years it took me to complete this work.

I want to thank my mentor and dear friend, Dr. John Moody. I benefited greatly from his wisdom. From his demand for details and documentation to the inclusion of specific topics, he gently guided and supported me through this process. I am deeply grateful.

I want to express my gratitude and appreciation to the "Bob Sikes Crew" Barbara Melton, Lanalda Wilson, Cyndee Laramore, and Doris Hilton for sharing with me their expertise in the field of teaching. To Lyn Stafford, one of many editors, thank you for challenging me to think and rewrite.

To Kathy White and Carol Mooso, two friends, who consistently "cheered me on" to finish the book. Thank you for your encouragement.

Z. Kunkel and S.R. Kunkel consistently shared their physical support and intellectual stimulation. Thank you to both of you.

Finally, to my mother, Flo McNames, and to my husband, Larry Kunkel, thank you both for encouraging me to grow and to succeed in the writing of this book. First, to my mother and loving friend, Flo (Mom), thank you for believing in me and encouraging me to never *give up* my dreams. And to my husband, Larry, thank you for sharing your love and companionship with me during the writing of this book and for helping me *fulfill* my dreams. Thank you, Mom, for giving me my roots. Thank you, Larry, for giving me my wings. I am most grateful.

The ABZ's of School Law for Teachers

Table of Contents

Chapter 1: Introduction

Every day a teacher may make as many as 300 decisions. Ninety-five per cent of them could deal with a possible legal issue! Very few teachers receive much training in legal matters as undergraduates. Most such courses occur in graduate school. Thus, the reason for this book is to give teachers an overview and working knowledge of legal matters that they may face in the world of education.

This book is **not** intended to give **any legal** advice. It is offered as a guidebook--to help you ask questions you may never have considered before becoming a teacher. Now as a teacher, you are swamped with the day to day responsibility of teaching.   When a legal issue arises, where do you go for help? Information in this book on local, state and federal policies and statutes **should** help you make a grounded decision in a given situation.

The topics in this book are explained within three sections: *awareness alert*, *balance out,* and *zero in.*

Each section will unlock the topic and guide you to find the answers to your questions. Understanding legal ramifications of your decisions will assist you in your teaching as well as safeguard your rights. Knowledge of the law can be a key to a successful career in education.

At **any** time in your teaching career, if you think you need legal advice, seek the counsel of a lawyer or a legal consultant immediately. An old proverb says: a man who is his own lawyer has a fool for a client.

Providing a Public School Education

Awareness Alert

Where is education mentioned in the U.S. Constitution? Although the term education is **not** specifically noted in the Constitution of the United States, the Constitution has been interpreted as to allow the United States Congress to raise and allocate money for education. Also, Congress can pass certain types of federal legislation that may affect schools.

The Bill of Rights is the name by which the first ten amendments to the United States Constitution are known. These first ten amendments were introduced by James Madison to the First United States Congress in 1789 as a series of articles. These articles were ratified by three-fourths of the then existing states in 1791 (Spaeth & Smith, 1991).

It is the Tenth Amendment to the U. S. Constitution

that *limits* the federal role in governing education (Imber & van Geel, 1995). The Tenth Amendment reserves *all powers* not granted to the federal government *to the citizenry or to the States*. This is the reason that the United States is one of the few countries in the world that *does not* have a centralized system of education.

Due to the Tenth Amendment, the largest majority of **statutes** controlling the operation of public schools are enacted by *state legislatures.* As the nineteenth century unfolded, the states began to pass state constitutions requiring that each of their state legislatures establish a system of free public schooling. Thus, 50 states equal 50 educational frameworks and 50 sets of state statutes and regulations.

Balance Out

Despite the Tenth Amendment and the *limits* placed on the federal government, federal statutes do provide an overreaching arch that states must follow when developing public educational policies. Two examples of federal legislation that impacts education immensely are the *Individuals with Disabilities Education Act* (*IDEA* was revised in 2004) and *No Child Left Behind* (*NCLB* passed in 2001). When amending *IDEA* in 2004, Congress added language to align it with the requirements of *NCLB* specifically in the area of special education standards. The effects of *NCLB* remain in flux today due to its complex requirements and its lack of funding by the federal government. Some states are even trying to remove themselves from *NCLB's legal requirements* because the federal funds are just not there (Siegel, 2009).

The U.S. Congress has great influence over public schools by controlling the *allocation of other federal funds* (for example Title I Funding). Federal statutes must mirror the U.S. Constitution. In addition, federal statutes are superior to all state law, including state constitutions.

As states have grappled with their educational policymaking, each **state's department of education** must develop its own plan to meet federal mandates. As these state plans trickle down, the local school district may interpret the state or federal policies and regulations the *same* **or** *differently*. Remember, what may be acceptable policy in one school district may not apply in the neighboring school district. So who *really* controls educational policymaking? Do not assume—ask.

Zero In

Today, not only do public and private schools exist, but also **charter** schools. Public charter schools are elementary or secondary schools in the United States that receive public money but have been freed from some of the rules, regulations, and statutes that apply to other public schools. This freedom from these governing rules is in exchange for agreeing to *achieve a specific type of accountability that produces specific* *results*. These accountabilities and results are set forth in the "charter" of that school (Nathan, 1996). Public charter schools are open to all and attended by choice.

While these charter schools provide an alternative to other public schools, they are part of the public education system and are not allowed to charge tuition. When enrollment in a public charter school reaches capacity, student admission is sometimes allocated by a lottery-based system or waiting lists.

Some private charter schools have been founded by teachers, parents or people who felt restricted by the "more traditional" public schools. State-authorized charters (schools not chartered by local school districts) are often established by non-profit groups, universities, government entities, and for-profit corporations (Eskenazi, 1999). Minnesota was the first state to pass a charter school law, in 1991. California was second, in 1992. As of 2009, 41 states and the District of Columbia have charter school laws (Center for Education Reform, 2009).

Key Vocabulary

Bill of Rights
Tenth Amendment
No Child Left Behind
Individuals with Disabilities Education Act
U.S. State Department of Education
State Departments of Education
Local School District
Charter Schools

Notes

Chapter 2: Getting Hired

Loyalty Oaths

Awareness Alert

Just as our elected officials are required to affirm their loyalty to the U.S. Constitution as they are sworn into office, some states mandate that prior to obtaining a teaching license the applicant must sign a similar loyalty oath. This requirement varies from state to state. Some courts have ruled that requiring teaching applicants to sign a loyalty oath may inhibit teachers from exercising their First Amendment right to their freedom of expression.

Balance Out

Two key U.S. Supreme Court cases are still at the heart of this debate. On the one hand in *Bagget v.*

Bullitt 377 U.S. 360 (1964), the Court forbids the use of vaguely worded loyalty oaths. On the other hand, in *Keyishian v. Board of Regents* 385 U.S. 589 (1967), the U.S. Supreme Court upheld certain New York state laws that required teachers to sign oaths. Do teachers have to affirm or pledge that they will uphold the Constitution of the United States and their respective state constitutions? If teachers must sign a loyalty oath, how and when does that occur?

Zero In

Does your state require you to sign a loyalty oath? One example of such an oath is one required of every person applying for a new teaching license or a renewal of a teaching license in an Indiana public school (McKinney, 1992). These applicants must sign an oath or affirm the following: "I solemnly swear (or affirm) that I will support the Constitution of the United States of America and the Constitution of the State of Indiana."

Reminder—always read a document **thoroughly** prior to signing.

Residency Requirements

Awareness Alert

You have applied to a school district for teaching positions that you are qualified for, and you have gone through the interview processes successfully. You have been recommended to the local school board for a teaching position and the school board has approved you for a teaching job. Congratulations! You have received notification that you have been hired by the Best School District in Public Schools, Any State, in the United States as a teacher.

Balance Out

Some states allow local school boards *to require* teachers to reside **within** the school district's boundaries as a condition of employment. Some states *prohibit* such a requirement.

Zero In

Does the local school district have the right to require you, a newly hired teacher, to live within the residential area of the school district? A residency clause should be located within the school district's policy manual and the school district's personnel department can obtain this information for you (McKinney, 1992).

If a residency clause exists, ask for a written copy of this policy and its residential boundaries. Moving from one school district to another may be a hardship to the families of some teachers. Check with the school district hiring you if there is a residency clause *prior to signing the contract.*

Individual Contracts

Awareness Alert

Most states have a uniform teaching contract that is prepared by their state departments of education. The contract that is entered into by a teacher and a school district should:

- be in writing
- be signed by both parties
- include the beginning date of the school year for teachers
- state the number of days teachers are required to work annually
- state the total salary to be paid and the number of salary payments to be made

Listed on your individual teacher's contract will be the number of days teachers are required to work annually. A beginning date will be listed but probably not an ending date. The reason for the lack of an ending date could be that you are in a district in which students may miss school days because of extreme weather conditions. Make sure that you ask what the *make-up policy for missing school days* is in your school district. With school accountability at such a high-stakes level, most state departments of education mandate a minimum number of student school days— how and when teachers and students make up the missed days is usually decided by the local school district. If unusual circumstances occur, make-up days may even be mandated by your state department of education. Prior knowledge is always a key to understanding!

Supplemental contracts may be added to your individual contract if you have agreed to a coaching duty, to extra-curricular service (i.e., yearbook advisor or club sponsor), to teach evening classes, summer school or to be a homebound tutor, to name just a few. These contracts may use different salary schedules. This important information should be a part of a master contract—an agreement between the teacher's collective bargaining unit and the school district. If the school district that has hired you does not have a master contract, your new school district's payroll or personnel department should have the information.

Balance Out

Usually, supplemental contracts are separate from the regular teacher's contract. For example, if you are hired as both a teacher and a coach, the supplemental contract for coaching could end or be withdrawn, but your regular teaching contract could remain intact.

Some states require that supplemental duty contracts *must* be separate from the basic teacher contract even if they are listed on the same document. If a state does not have a statute that divides the contracts, then the separateness of the contracts *depends on the policy of the school district.*

Zero In

Ask if your teaching contract and the supplemental contracts you are signing are separate or linked. Also, make sure that date and *time* you originally signed the contracts are listed on the documents, because in cases of a "reduction in force" or layoff, many master contracts usually require that the reduction process be based on seniority in the teacher's area of certification.

Teachers who have the same areas of certification and the same number of years of service have been subjected to having their positions eliminated by using a deck of cards. In one instance, several teachers had signed their original teaching contracts on the same date of a specific year. The time they signed their contracts *was not* listed. Because these teachers had signed on the same date and year, they were given a deck of cards, and the teacher that drew the lowest card was now unemployed. Make sure that not only the *date* of your signature is on your contract, but also the *time*.

Collective Bargaining Statutes and Teacher Unions

Awareness Alert

Currently 33 states have a state policy that authorizes some form of collective negotiations between teachers and local school boards (AFL/CIO, Public Employee Department, 1997). The definition of *collective bargaining* is the process in which a teacher's union represents and negotiates for all the teachers in the district at the same time. The agreements that are reached through this bargaining process are listed in a document usually called a *master contract*. Master contracts are a district level document and are distributed by the local school district.

Although some states that may not have passed a law requiring some type of collective bargaining, may have established a *precedent* of collective bargaining. Agreements may have been made between the local school board and a group of teachers out of *good faith.*

It is essential that you know if your state has a public law addressing collective bargaining. Collective bargaining statutes can affect your status as a teacher—so can the *lack* of collective bargaining statutes. Ask if your state is one of the thirty-three states that have a collective bargaining law (AFL/CIO, Public Employee Department (1997). If the answer is yes, determine who is covered by the law and who is excluded. In some states supervisory staff, superintendents, principals and even part-time staff are not covered and are excluded from the bargaining process.

Balance Out

There are four basic types of unions. The first two are usually associated with industry employees, but may exist in a public school setting. One type of union is a *union* shop. This type of union requires prospective employees either to already be or to become a union member upon becoming employed.

The second type of union, a *closed* shop, mandates that prior to the hiring of a person they must already be a member of the union. Usually these unions are industry or trade unions.

The third example of a union is called an *agency* shop. When you are hired as an employee, you must either join the union or if you decline union membership, you may have to pay what is known as *fair share dues*. Fair share dues means that as a nonmember, the employee must pay the same fees that a union member pays minus the political action committee (PAC) fees. Legally, unions cannot require you to pay for any of their political action contributions.

The fourth type of union does not mandate membership in the union or the payment of fair share dues. Twenty-one states currently have a *right to work* law. In these states such laws **prevent** collective bargaining agreements from issuing union security clauses that require teachers to support and or share the costs of union representation.

There are two *national* teacher unions that state and/or local teachers' associations (unions) may join. They are *the National Education Association* (NEA) and the *American Federation of Teachers* (AFT). Determine to which national union (if any) your school district belongs.

Your school district may be independent of ties to any *official* national or state teachers' association or union. Affiliations with two unions may even exist within the same school district and could alternate yearly as one becomes the controlling union based on membership. It is imperative that you have *all* the information available on unions and union membership for your school district.

Zero In

Prior to signing your teaching contract, ask the

school district that is about to hire you if you must join a union. Regardless of the answer, ask to be informed of all of the options that apply to you. Inquire which national union the local teachers' association belongs-- if any--and does this state have a *right to work law.*

Always request the information regarding the fees. Most fair share fees are just as much as union membership dues, but may be $50 to $100 less.

*Remember: the master contract booklet that you will be given is a **must read.*** This booklet will be given to you from your local school district's personnel office. In this document will be a wealth of information: number of sick leave days allowed, bereavement leave, grievance procedures, the teacher evaluation process and timeline, sick leave banks, and salary schedules just to name a few. If you do not have to join the union, what are your rights as *a nonunion member*? **Ask**.

Work Slowdowns, Stoppages and Strikes

Awareness Alert

You have been on the job for one week. The contract you were hired under is the most recent contract ratified by the local teacher's union and the school board—it may be last year's contract or one agreed upon even three years ago or more. All of the teachers, including you, in the district remain under a *status-quo* agreement until a new contract is approved by the school board and the teacher's union. Status-quo means that teachers are working under the last master contract that was approved by the school board and the local teacher's union.

The teacher's union in your local school district is calling for a work stoppage due to the fact that the bargaining process for this year's contract has stalled or is at an impasse. An impasse in the bargaining setting means that both sides have reached a *standstill* in the bargaining process. The administrators (representing the local school board) and the team of teachers (representing the local teacher's union) have both stated that neither side can continue any farther with this process.

Procedures that most collective bargaining states have in place to break an impasse are mediation, fact-finding hearings, and arbitration. A third party, a mediator, fact-finder or an arbitrator, is brought in (usually from the state's employment relations board) to settle the conflict. Each third-party person or persons brought in must be neutral. The items that can not be resolved (usually *money* items at this point) become the focus.

First, in *mediation*, a mediator from the state meets with each side separately and tries to bring both sides together through compromise. If this method does not work, then *fact-finding hearings* begin.

During this second step, each side is required to submit whatever information they may possess to support their position for the unresolved items to this third party, the fact finder. After reviewing all the data, the fact finder renders a decision. Both sides may agree to accept the judgment, but they are not required to do so.

The third phrase of this system is *arbitration*. Again, a third party examines all the documents and issues a ruling. If a state has a *binding arbitration* law then both sides **must** accept the ruling. If the state does not, neither side *has* to agree. The bargaining process ends and the situation resorts back to an impasse in which teachers are still working under the last contract that was ratified—the status quo contract.

Balance Out

At this writing, twenty-four states prohibit strikes by teachers and nine states allow them. Any organized work stoppages, slowdowns or refusals to work can be considered a strike. If an organized work slowdown, refusal to work or work stoppage occurs, many penalties can result such as fines, loss of pay, legal fees, the loss of a teaching position, or even imprisonment. Currently twelve states impose a range of these penalties. Striking unions may be required to reimburse the school district for expenses that the school district may have incurred during a work-related slowdown.

Zero In

Is your state one of the few states that allows teachers the right to strike? If it is not, consider what could happen to your job if you participate in a slowdown, work stoppage, or strike. School boards have filed court injunctions ordering striking teachers back to work.

As an illegally striking teacher, you could be terminated based upon the fact that you *abandoned your job*. If the courts concurred, you would not have any *procedural due process* options or rights of recourse.

Procedural due process is a state policy that

requires local school districts to provide teachers with prior written notification of the cancellation of a contract and a right to a hearing. Each state's due process policy will have provisions that vary based on the teacher's length of service and fitness to teach to name only a few.

If you do not participate in the slowdown, work stoppage or strike--and you try to cross a picket line— it may become very unpleasant. **Weigh your decisions carefully**.

Thirty-three states have made some type of decision to allow teachers the right to strike or not to strike. What have the remaining seventeen states decided? As a teacher, you must know the answer.

Key Vocabulary

Loyalty Oaths
Residency Requirements
Individual Contracts
Supplemental Contracts
Make-up Policy for Missed School Days
Collective Bargaining Process
Master Contract
Unions
Right to Work Law
Status-quo Agreement
Impasse
Mediation
Fact-finding
Arbitration
Work Slowdowns, Stoppages, and Strikes

Notes

Chapter 3: School Safety

Daily Safety Standards and Crisis Planning
Awareness Alert

Public schools are a *mirror* of society. Whatever situation is out of control in our society is reflected in our schools. Two of the most recent examples of such out-of-control occurrences are drugs and violence (Smith, 1997). The *most* critical and important assignment that an educator has *every day* is protecting the health, safety and welfare of the students and all of the school personnel.

In 1970 the United States Congress passed and enacted the Occupational Safety and Health Act, which created the *Occupational Safety and Health Administration (OSHA)* under the Department of Labor. This public law was amended in 2004.

This law requires every employer to furnish each of its employees a place of employment that is free from recognized hazards that are causing or are likely to cause death or serious physical harm. Each employee is required by this act to comply with occupational safety and health standards and all rules, regulations and orders issued pursuant to this act.

Balance Out

Most school districts define a crisis as *any* situation that threatens the safety and well-being of the school, students or staff--either physically or emotionally. Every teacher (regardless of full-time, part-time, temporary or substitute status) *must know* the crucial components of a school's safety plan. Before ever entering a classroom, critical information should be reviewed, which include, but is not limited to:

- map of the school building
- list of codes—silent codes, color codes and/or signals
- all evacuation procedures
- identification of school areas that could be used as crisis centers (including alternatives)
- lock down procedures
- specific procedural actions related to such

occurrences as fires, tornadoes, hurricanes, earthquakes.

All regular teachers (full-time, part-time or temporary) should be familiar with the *entire* school safety plan (Checklist for a Safe and Secure School Environment, 1999). *Every teacher and staff member of the school* must know the location of fire hydrants, power boxes, circuit breakers, gas and plumbing controls. In addition, *everyone* should know how to access all existing emergency telephones or communication systems, the location of any special programs housed in the building such as early childhood or special needs and **basic first aid**. Several staff members should be licensed to perform CPR— know who these people *are*.

The school principal and the school's crisis team are usually the first responders. However, if they are directly involved in the incident then *you*, the teacher, may be the one needed to turn the water and gas off. **Always expect the unexpected and be ready**.

As educators you already know that school safety

and security extend beyond the boundaries of the school campus. Thinking about safety issues as *interior* or *exterior* school building situations should assist you in complying with all safety guidelines.

Interior safety concerns—what happens *inside* the building-- should include (but are not limited to):

- unscheduled fire, severe weather related, lock-down, or other drills
- actual fire, severe weather related, or lock-down incidents
- bomb threats or scares
- classroom/school-wide power outages
- on-site pranks and vandalism
- tragic death of a student or staff member on school property
- incident of school violence (including possession of weapons)
- dangerous person on school property
- suicide threat, attempt, or completion
- environmental hazard or spill on school property
- hostage or abduction incident on school property
- contagious disease
- cult or gang activity within the school or on school property.

40

Exterior safety—what happens on a community wide basis--should include (but are not limited to):

- severe weather related incidents
- lock-down incidents
- school bus accident
- tragic death of a student or staff member off school property
- cluster of suicide threats, attempts, or completion
- environmental hazard or spill in the community
- hostage, abduction, or robbery in the community—the perpetrator may possibly be seeking refuge in a school
- contagious disease threat in the community
- community or political protest activity in the community
- cult or gang altercations off campus
- an act of terrorism, declaration of war, or another major national incident.

All schools should have some type of **Crisis Plan** or **School Safety Handbooks** in place (Whitaker, 1998). These action plans should be standardized and consistent in format so they can be easily followed.

All teachers and staff members of a building must know this information and must practice the procedures. Some school districts require parts of the **Crisis Plan** or **School Safety Handbook** to be posted throughout the building for substitutes and visitors.

A plan only provides guidelines by which to operate and a starting point for taking control of the crisis situation. No two crises are ever the same, and no plan, no matter how well prepared it is, will address every single aspect of the incident. A crisis may not be avoidable, but it may be controlled correctly if the right decisions are made and the right actions are taken early.

Zero In

Teachers who are instructing in areas that are near hazards, such as any machinery, chemicals or potentially dangerous equipment in their classrooms, have additional safety concerns. These areas can include but are not limited to industrial arts, vocational education, art rooms, and science laboratories. Any classroom may become a dangerous environment, but teachers in such potentially hazardous areas *must* take extra precautions.

To begin, these teachers should have a classroom *safety contract*. This contract should be the content of the first instructional lesson of the school year and repeated often. Each student and parent or guardian must sign and date this document prior to participating in the class. The original copy should remain in the teacher's files and a duplicate copy placed in the administrative office.

Once you have instructed your students about this contract and it has been signed, then an exam should be given on its provisions. Any student not passing the exam should be reinstructed and retested. Only students passing the safety exam should be allowed to use chemicals or equipment. No exceptions allowed.

In addition, the following tips for teachers are *strongly suggested*:

- Demonstrate the **safe** use of equipment or

machinery.

- Teach and **reteach** the safety classroom rules throughout the school year.
- **Post** the safety school rules several places in the classroom.
- Utilize **safe** and effective supervision procedures.
- Supply safety devices (such as goggles, eye wash stations) and train students on their proper usage.
- Warn students constantly of potential **foreseeable** dangers.
- Practice steps to take if an accident should occur.
- Complete and document routine safety checks of lab equipment, machinery, chemicals, physical education equipment, outside ground equipment.
- If chemicals are in the classroom, they should be arranged by chemical families, not alphabetically, and stored in a locked, ventilated location so only authorized personnel may open and enter.
- If live animals are housed in any classrooms, safety rules should be posted that include proper animal care instructions.
- All parents or guardians should have notification of live animals housed within the school building.
- The local fire marshal or fire department should

be given annually a current list of live animals and chemicals, including their exact location in the building in case of a fire.

- Aid ill or injured students **immediately and properly**.
- Be trained **yourself** in safety precautions and first aid.

For those students *not* willing to follow the *safety contract*, a parent conference should be initiated immediately. The projected outcome of this meeting is to ensure that the student will conform to the procedures listed on the safety contract. If this objective is not reached, then the administration should, as a suggestion, withdraw the student from the class and issue a failing grade to the student. This may seem harsh, but the safety of all students and staff must be one of the highest priorities in a school every day.

Being proactive and safety conscience will only enhance a safe learning environment for your students and all staff members. School safety is **no** accident.

Reporting Child Neglect and Abuse

Awareness Alert

The Child Abuse Prevention and Treatment Acts (CAPTA) were established by the United States Congress in 1974. These acts have been amended several times and were reauthorized in 2003 by the *Keeping Children and Families Safe Act*. These acts have *required* each state to pass a mandatory reporting law for child abuse and neglect. Fifty different states mean 50 different wordings and requirements.

Balance Out

The first day you are hired as a teacher, ask the principal for a copy of your state's statute and/or ask for a copy of the policy for the school and district for reporting child abuse or neglect.

Always remember that we, as teachers, *only* report a possibility of child abuse or suspected neglect. The proper authorities make the determination or judgment to investigate. In this age of technology, the proper authorities have access to much more information on specific families than we have as teachers regarding child abuse or neglect reporting.

For example, a family may have moved from state to state to avoid retribution from various reports of abuse or neglect. This report may be the one that saves a child's life or this may be the first report of an incident, and this intervention, with the family, may prevent further incidents.

On the one hand, when a teacher makes a report (or any citizen for that matter), the reporter is anonymous. If done in good faith, the reporter has immunity from civil and criminal liability. On the other hand, any person who *knowingly fails* to make a report under his or her state statute requirements may be *eligible for conviction of a crime*.

Zero In

Here are some questions that as a teacher you should ask:

- **Who** does the law require to make a report? Most statutes require "any person who has reason to believe…" must report.

- **What** is the meaning of abuse or neglect? Laws may include definitions such as "a child (usually under 18) in risk of (physical or emotional) harm, sexual abuse, exploitation, or death."

- **What** does *reason to believe* mean? It usually means that any person who has evidence that, if presented to individuals of similar background and training, would believe that a child was abused or neglected. Evidence may be physical or verbal.

- Are **teachers** held to a higher standard to report? Usually yes. State statutes also require teachers additionally to immediately notify the individual in charge of the school. This notified individual must make a report or cause a report to be made.

- **What** if the individual in charge does not make

the report and instructs you, the teacher, not to notify the proper authorities? If no report was made, the teacher **is not** relieved of the obligation to report.

- **Who** are the proper authorities that receive the report? Each school should have a very close working relationship with the local child protective service agency. If this agency is not available, notify the local law enforcement agency or the county prosecutor. Most states now have a hotline for reporting child abuse and neglect. Many times a verbal report is all that is necessary.

Remember, teachers **only report**; the proper authorities make the determination to investigate.

At this point, the **unthinkable must** be mentioned. As a teacher and an adult, you are **responsible** for the education and the safety of your students who are children regardless of their age. As their teacher, **do not** ever place yourself in a position of compromise with a child. Time and time again, media coverage has shown teachers behaving inappropriately with their students. Do not be alone in a one-to-one situation with a student. Do not use language that is suggestive in any improper or sexual way. Do not touch any child in an inappropriate manner. In essence, as their teacher, **do not** become the **child abuser**.

As a child abuser, a teacher not only steals the innocence of the child but damages the trust the child has not only for his or her self but also in others in positions of authority. The child will feel as if he or she is to blame for these acts and then feel guilty for them having occurred. These children experience thoughts of being broken and feel they are damaged goods—thus many are incapable of having a healthy view of sexuality as an adult. The child's life will **never** be the same—as a child or an adult.

This educator of thirty-seven years has witnessed teachers being handcuffed, arrested and taken to jail for child abuse charges. Educators that commit these acts of violence toward their students are pedophiles and at the minimum should lose their teaching licenses and then be prosecuted to the fullest extent of the law. It is **imperative** as teachers and administrators that if we suspect a fellow educator of child abuse, we notify the authorities immediately. Teachers should not have to *police their own ranks*, but in the case of child abuse regardless of in-school or out-of-school—teachers must do what is **best for kids—always.**

Confidentiality of Student Records

Awareness Alert

All states have public record laws known as *freedom of information laws* or *sunshine laws*. These laws permit public access of public records including some documents within school districts without parental consent. A school district should have a formal definition in place for the freedom of information or sunshine law as required by that specific state. In addition, guidelines should be in place to provide open meetings and to handle disclosure of any of this public information. Depending on the type of request, most of the time this is done at the district level. For example, a newspaper may be requesting a compilation of test scores by schools--not sorted by student names--over a specific time span. These sorts of questions are directed to the district administrators.

The Family Educational Rights and Privacy Act of 1974 (FERPA) applies to all institutions, public or private, that receive federal funding (all public schools do receive some type of federal funding). FERPA was created to *protect the privacy* of student records, provide for the *inspection* of these records, the right to *seek to amend* these records and *to limit the disclosure* of these records to third parties.

Balance Out

What are considered educational records? Educational records include the following: directory information, special education records, test data and assessments, grades, discipline referrals, medical and health records, reports and evaluations from external agencies, and information on any medium that can identify an individual student such as a DVD, CD, video, audio, photograph or any electronic file.

Who has the right to review these educational records? Parents (including non-custodial parents), and legal guardians all have the right to review the educational records as defined in the FERPA definition. All school personnel who have *legitimate educational interests* maintain the right to review the records. The parental and legal guardian rights to review records and to ask that an educational record be amended transfers to the student when he or she reaches the age of 18 or attends a school beyond the high school level. Students to whom the FERPA rights have been transferred are known as eligible students.

Zero In

Requests to review educational records by out-of-school person(s) should be completed in writing and given to the local school's administrative office. It is imperative to verify the identification of the person(s) making the request. In this time of identity theft and child abductions, information should never be released without the proper confirmation.

For the out-of-school person(s) requesting a review, the school must disclose the records within a 45 day time limit. This 45 day window provides the school the opportunity to ensure proper identification of the credentials of the person(s) making the request. Schools are *not* required to make copies of the records unless the person requesting the records cannot come to the school for a legitimate reason (e.g. a noncustodial parent who lives in another city).

School personnel who have legitimate educational interests may review a student's records in a less formal process. Usually filed in each student's record is a "review of record" sheet. Educators are asked to provide a signature, date, time, and the reason the review was made. Some school districts require that the student's permanent record remain in the office area—some may allow the file to be removed and taken to the classroom. **Always ask what the proper procedure is for school personnel to review educational records.**

Information that can be removed from a student's

educational record *prior* to review is any information regarding another student. Names of other students should never be included in another student's file. If any financial records of the student's parents are in the educational record, they may also be removed before disclosure.

A student's educational record does not have to include any personal notes or files made by teachers or other school faculty if these files have been kept separately and privately in the teacher's or faculty's private files and in their sole possession. All entries made to a student's official educational record should always be *objective, correct, concise, dated, and completed in a professional manner.*

Protecting the confidentiality of student records is a very complex situation. All requests for review (especially subpoenas, court orders, and requests from law enforcement agencies) should be directed to the office staff. They have the knowledge when, what, and how to share this information. It is crucial that all school personnel be trained to ensure the importance of confidentiality of student's records. Even comments made to third parties regarding the content of a student's file on such topics as test scores, behavior, or medication, could become a FERPA violation.

Improper disclosure of information is a breach of the student's privacy. As a result of the decision in the *Gonzaga University v. Doe,* 536. U.S. 273 (2002) court case, a Family Policy Compliance Office (FPCO) has been established within the FERPA Act. This *federal office* has set forth procedures for resolving student or parent complaints about suspected FERPA violations. Students or parents must first file a written complaint with FPCO. If the FPCO determines that the written complaint information is timely and has merit, the FPCO will decide to initiate an investigation.

First, FPCO will notify the educational institution involved of the charge. Second, a written response will be requested from this educational institution concerning the charge. If the FPCO determines a violation has occurred, the FPOC distributes a notice of "factual findings" and a statement of specific steps that the institution must take to comply with FERPA.

Dispensing Medications to Students

Awareness Alert

Today, a high percentage of students are taking medications, and that number appears to be rising. Many students must take medications during the school day. Who should administer and monitor these medications? Obviously, the school nurse should be doing this task. What if the school nurse is on leave or the school doesn't have a nurse or nurse's aide on site? Who then is responsible for dispensing the medication or providing the medical services?

The National Education Association (NEA), one of the largest teacher's unions in the country, has a policy recommending that "only medical personnel should be required to administer" prescribed medication or perform medical services in schools. In addition, the NEA believes that teachers should have the right to refuse to administer medications or perform medical services without fear of repercussion (Jehen, 2008).

What is the policy of your school district for teachers on dispensing medications or performing medical services?

Balance Out

Some school districts have policies stating that principals select two or more support staff or paraprofessionals to be trained to perform these duties if the school cannot provide a school nurse. Duties may include (but are not limited to) giving-over-the-counter medications, prescribed medications, cleaning tracheas, administering oxygen, nebulizers, inhalers, and administering medication with self-administered epinephrine devices like Epi pins for allergic reactions.

For most schools, the medication policies in place include very strict procedures. For example, usually all medications must be brought to the school by a parent or guardian. Some schools allow the dispensing of over-the-counter medications, some do not. Dispensing prescription medications may require a written statement from the parent or legal guardian and from the physician. Also, prescription medications must be in the original bottle or container, which must have the student's name, current prescription information (medication name, dose and directions), and a current date. Trained staff should verify that the substance in the container is the actual medication listed by consulting the Prescribed Drug Report. Since pharmacies are using so many generic forms of medication, schools may include using an online service to verify the medications. When verified, the medication should be placed under lock and key in the administrative office or nursing station. Some schools do permit students to carry certain medications on their person such as inhalers and diabetic monitoring meters.

Zero In

Unfortunately, mix-ups and mistakes happen. In one case, a student was given the proper dose of medication at school. The student passed out and after he was rushed to the hospital it was discovered that "someone at home" had been double dosing the child all weekend. It only took one dose from the school to *overdose* him. In this lawsuit, the school was found not liable or negligent.

In another situation, a teacher was taking the class on a field trip and agreed to dispense the medication. The student pretended to take the medication (put it in his/her mouth, but did not swallow), went to the restroom, and gave it to another student. The receiving student went into convulsions. The school was negligent because this should have been foreseeable to the teachers involved (more on torts, lawsuits, and liability in Chapter 8).

A teacher's responsibility *is* to teach. Along with that responsibility is the expectation that teachers provide a safe learning environment. However, teachers must protect themselves, and you should know your rights. Check with the principal and the teacher's union to see what your requirements are in dispensing medications and in providing specific medical services.

This is not a suggestion, but a warning. A teacher should never make a recommendation to a parent or guardian to place a student on a medication for any condition. In the past, teachers have suggested to parents that students be medicated for Attention Deficient Disorder or Attention Deficient Hyperactivity Disorder to just name a few medical conditions. As a teacher, you may certainly suggest that the parent consult their physician regarding areas of concern for a specific child. However, *never* should you as the teacher *prescribe a medication.* In this extremely hazardous area of dispensing medications and administering medical services, always err on the side of safety for your students and yourself.

Key Vocabulary

Occupational Safety and Health Act
School Safety Plan or Handbook
School Crisis Plans
Interior Building Safety Issues
Exterior Building Safety Issues
Safety Contracts for Students
Child Abuse Prevention and Treatment Act
Keeping Children and Families Safe Act
Freedom of Information Laws or Sunshine Laws
Family Educational Rights and Privacy Act
Family Policy Compliance Office

Notes

Chapter 4: As a Teacher: Am I Too Strict or Not Strict Enough?

Student Rights

Awareness Alert

Today, more than 200 years after its passage in 1791, the First Amendment continues to be one of the bedrocks of freedom for the United States. The freedom of religion, speech, press, assembly and petition are fundamental rights offered to citizens under this amendment. The First Amendment applies to all levels of government, including public schools (Haynes et al. 2003). Courts have permitted school officials *under some circumstances* to limit or monitor these freedoms of students.

With the First Amendment being the cornerstone of specific guaranteed freedoms, additional court cases and landmark acts have immeasurably influenced the public schools. *Brown v. Board of Education*, 347

U.S. 483 (1954) attacked the *separate but equal doctrine.* The U.S. Supreme Court in this case declared *that in public education* separate but equal has no right to exist. Public schools segregated by race are unconstitutional.

Another act, known as the *Civil Rights Act* of 1964 has also impacted schools. This law clearly prohibits discrimination in the areas of race, national origin, gender, and religion; and the law applies to any agency or program that receives federal funding. Since almost *all* public schools receive some level of federal funding, the effect of this act is wide spread.

Specifically two provisions under the *Civil Rights Acts* of 1964, Title VII and Title IX, afford students *antidiscrimination* rights. Title VII sets forth that "no person in the United States shall, on the grounds of race, color, or national origin, be excluded from participation in, or denied the benefits of, or be subjected to discrimination under *any* program or activity receiving federal funds."

Title IX mirrors Title VII and declares that "no

person in the United States shall, on the basis of sex (gender) be excluded from participation in, or denied the benefits of, or be subjected to discrimination under any *education program or activity* that receives federal funds. Both Title VII and Title IX include public schools, but Title IX specifically mentions education.

In 1982, the U.S. Supreme Court decided that *undocumented* (illegal immigrant) *children* have a constitutional right to receive a free K-12 public education. In this case, *Plyler v. Doe*, 457 U.S. 202 (1982), the U.S. Supreme court found that Texas violated the Equal Protection Clause of the Fourteenth Amendment by denying these undocumented children a K-12 public education. Reasoning that such *children* are in the United States through no fault of their own, the Court determined these children are entitled to the same K-12 education that the state provides to children who are citizens or legal residents (Vock, 2007). Continuing through today, litigation and court decisions have embraced the rights of public school students. As their teacher, it is essential that you understand *their* rights as well.

Balance Out

The First Amendment states that the government **may not** *establish* religion. What does this mean for students who attend a public school or are in attendance at a public school-sponsored activity? The **Establishment Clause** often referred to as the separation of church and state, is more strictly followed in a public school setting for two reasons: (1) students are impressionably young people, and (2) they are a *captive audience* when required by the state to attend a public school (Haynes et al. 2003).

Students do have the right to pray alone or within a group and to discuss their faith with other students, as long as their actions do not interfere with the school's activity or force other students to participate (*Settle v. Dickson County School Board*, 53 F.3d 152 (6th Cir. 1995), cert. denied, 516 U. S. 989 (1995). Also, students may express their religious ideas in class assignments or discussions if it is pertinent to the subject and meets the requirement for the assignment (*Cole v. Oroville Union High School*, 229 F.3d 1092 (9th Cir. 2000).

In the area of freedom of speech or expression, one of the most important points to be cognizant of as a new teacher emerges from the statement of Justice Abe Fortas from the U.S. Supreme Court ruling in the *Tinker v. Des Moines Independent Community School District*, 393 U.S. 503 (1969). He stated "neither teachers nor students shed their constitutional rights to freedom of speech or expression at the schoolhouse gate." The ruling of this famous case, decided in 1975, created what is now known as the *Tinker Test*. Through this court case, the U.S. Supreme Court recognized that the constitutional freedoms of students and teachers must remain intact at school unless there is a constitutionally valid reason for the specific regulation of speech.

In regard to students, schools can only regulate

student speech or expression to the extent that the regulation is *needed*. To apply the *Tinker Test*, at least one of two scenarios must be present. First, schools may moderate a situation to prevent a "material and substantial" disruption of the educational process. Or second, schools may control an occurrence to "protect the rights of others within the school community." However, there is an important condition to remember here. School authorities *cannot* override student speech or expression just because the school authorities disagree. So, how do schools *balance* the rights of students as citizens under the First Amendment with the need to maintain an orderly environment?

Zero In

As mentioned, the U.S. Supreme Court in the Tinker case clarified that students do not shed their freedom of speech or expression rights at the schoolhouse door. So, what is the definition of student speech or expression? The definition of *speech* or *expression* that the courts typically use is (1) that there is intent to convey a specific message present and (2) this message can be understood by those who view it.

There are three classifications of student speech: private on campus speech, curriculum-based speech, and off campus non-school sponsored speech. The first type of speech, private, occurs at school, but is not sponsored by the school. For example, this communication by students takes place at lunch in the cafeteria, in the hallways or locker bays. The second type, curriculum-based, is student speech that transpires as part of the school program. The third, off campus speech, is non-school sponsored student speech that happens away from school property. What do most public schools regulate and how do they achieve their goals?

Prior to attending a school, students should be given the school's Code of Conduct. This Code of Conduct should detail the expectations of student behavior, the required standards of the school and the consequences for not following these rules. *Private, non-school sponsored on campus speech* should be discussed in these regulations. Schools have set in place their expectations of students and the rules and regulations that will aide them in this responsibility.

Acceptable *curriculum-based* school sponsored speech is based upon *Bethel School District No. 403 v. Fraser,* 478 U.S. 675 (1986). This U.S. Supreme Court ruling says that schools are responsible for teaching the *habits of civility* and thus could *prohibit the use of vulgar and offensive terms.*

The court has also stated that the content of school-sponsored newspapers, yearbooks, and websites can be regulated (*Hazelwood School District v. Kuhlmeier,* 484 U.S. 260 (1988). The courts have determined that these publications are an extension of the classroom and can be controlled in regards to style and content.

In most all school-sponsored activities, school regulations of speech may also extend to obscene or defamatory instances. Schools *may* override student speech or expression in racially, ethnically, sexist, or politically tense situations.

Students requesting the right to distribute religious materials fall into the categories listed above as well as under the regulation of "time, manner and place." School officials may also manage student requests for rallies and demonstrations. Orderly use of school facilities and maintaining the non-interruption of the school day can be controlled by the school. Again, just using the argument of school authority **disagreement** with the ideas should not stop the students' rights to freedom of association or cause its censorship.

The issue of individuality verses conformity comes into play with the subject of dress codes or uniforms. Unless uniforms are required, a student's clothing or "dress" is *usually* given wide latitude as long as long as the dress is considered not disruptive. Illegal substances to minors cannot be advertised on a t-shirt, article of clothing or backpack. For example, any speech that advocates drugs, alcohol or tobacco may be halted. Gang dress or gang signals are not usually allowable.

Non-school sponsored speech or expressions (those that occur off school premises i.e. student home web pages) are more difficult to balance. School officials usually have the authority to apply the school's discipline rules in these cases if:

*the student conduct off the school grounds is unlawful

*the student conduct may *reasonably* be considered interference with school purposes or an educational function

*the student handbook contains the statement that such unlawful conduct even when occurring as non-school sponsored speech and occurring off school property is a basis for suspension or expulsion.

All students (and staff) are entitled to a safe public school environment. Student speech is entitled to First Amendment protection within the boundaries listed above.

Student Conduct and Discipline

Prior to the 1960s, schools operated under in loco parentis, a belief that provided schools the same broad authority as parents. Due to the Tinker case and other acts, schools must recognize that, although a child's legal status is not the same as an adults, a child is constitutionally protected. Because the child is legally a child, not an adult, the schools are justified in exercising more control over their students. Instead of in loco parentis, today schools use the *Tinker Test* to monitor the "time, place, and manner" of their students' activities. The Tinker case ruling greatly impacts schools.

School authorities must use *lawful* controls which mean they may manage a student's action when control is necessary. A school must protect people or property, promote learning, and prevent the disruption of the educational environment. The fundamental meaning of *lawful* is that schools can only utilize as much rulemaking and punishing as is required to establish the school's goals.

Balance Out

All schools should require *equal* treatment of all enrolled students in a school. To achieve this goal, students must be notified *in advance* of behavior that is unacceptable so they have the opportunity to comply with the required school standards. Thus, distribution of school rules and regulations are a must *prior* to a student's attendance. Usually these *guides or handbooks* are dispersed during registration.

Classroom rules should be set prior to the opening of a school year and must work in concert with the overreaching school rules and regulations. Individual teachers will enhance their pre-established codes of conduct by using the first days of class to teach not only their classroom rules, but also the school's rules and regulations.

Some school districts require parents to sign a statement that they and their children have received and understand the rules and regulations. Check with your new school district for its copy of the board's conduct policy, the school's approved rules and regulations, and any disciplinary forms that you may be required to complete if an infraction occurs in your classroom or during hall monitor duty or on bus duty (just to name a few places that may require a teacher's monitoring).

Zero In

Disciplining students is a very complex issue. When enforcing rules or regulations, some situations can escalate very quickly. Education is a property and liberty right for students. These rights are provided and protected by the Fourteenth Amendment (1868): "nor shall any State deprive any person of life, liberty, or property without the due process of law." Due process entitles students an opportunity to voice their version of an incident either prior to a suspension or expulsion or within a reasonable amount of time thereafter.

School officials are usually the ones who insure that the due process is implemented. Many times the discipline form includes a place for the teacher to list the infraction (always be specific) and which school rule or state statute this infraction violated. In addition, forms usually include a space for the person in charge of school-wide discipline to list the comments of the student.

Due process also protects the liberty interest of a student (a student's reputation). Serious charges can damage the student's reputation as well as interfere with future educational and employment opportunities. Building due process procedures into the discipline process is one way to ensure that each student is afforded the chance to give his/her side of the incident.

Another predicament that can be magnified quickly is a *theft, suspicion of alcohol, cigarettes, drugs or weapons* in a school that may require a *search and thus a seizure.* The Fourth Amendment (1791) provides students the right "to be secure in their persons, house, papers, and effects against unreasonable searches and seizures, and no warrants shall be issued, but upon probable cause." In these situations schools are held to a slightly lower standard—instead of *probable cause*, schools only need a *reasonable cause.* Too many teachers have taken it upon themselves to investigate a situation that happens in their classrooms and have been sued or lost their jobs as a result of an *improper* search or seizure. Examples of an *improper* search may be "patting a student down" incorrectly on his or her body or continuing a search when the contraband is found.

The Fourth Amendment also prohibits blanket searches (the search of a group of students, several desks, backpacks or lockers) when it states "and particularly describing the *place* to be searched and the *persons or things* to be seized." This is not advice, but a warning. Do not **ever** *remove the clothing of a student to search for anything.*

School officials are trained in the proper way to search students and what legally they can and cannot do on school property. The issue of a search or seizure should always be resolved by a school official.

As of this writing thirty states have now banned the use of corporal punishment in public schools. The Eighth Amendment (1791) comes to the forefront when excessive force is used in schools. The amendment states that "nor can cruel and unusual punishments be inflicted." Can paddling or corporal punishment constitute cruel and unusual punishment?

Thirty states believe that it does. If your school district allows this type of punishment, again, school administrative officials *should be the ones to administer it—not teachers.* If corporal punishment is used, litigation may result even if corporal punishment is permissible by a state or district statute.

As school district employees, teachers do have the authority and should take steps as necessary to control the disorderly conduct of students in all situations and places that fall under the jurisdiction of the school district. Teachers should also take charge when this conduct interferes with the educational program of the schools or threatens the health and safety of others. How far should discipline measures go? Suggestions are:

*the punishment administered should match the level of the infraction.

*the punishment should be related to the need to maintain an orderly school environment conducive to learning.

*the school district employee should not discriminate among students.

*the school district employee should not demean or degrade students privately or publicly.

*the school district employee should not violate any individual rights constitutionally guaranteed to students.

Teachers should know the school district's rules for students regarding attendance and discipline. Ask if the school district has in place policies on zero-tolerance for such things as fighting, weapons or drug. If zero-tolerance policies do not exist, then what are the policies for drugs, weapons, fighting, and academic penalties to name a few? Know before you proceed.

Key Vocabulary

First Amendment, 1791
Civil Rights Act of 1964
Establishment Clause
Tinker Test
Time, Manner, and Place
Fourteenth Amendment, 1868
Education is a Property and Liberty Right for Students
Due Process
Fourth Amendment, 1791
Eighth Amendment, 1791
Corporal Punishment

Notes

Chapter 5: The Students' Know Their Legal Rights, But What Are Mine?

Teacher Rights

Awareness Alert

Remember that "students do not shed their rights at the school house gate" and neither do teachers. However, there are special circumstances when a public school has the need to balance the right of its employees to promote the school's goals. Prior to the 1960s, being hired as a teacher was considered a *privilege* rather than a right. Back then, teachers had basically no First Amendment, Fourth Amendment, or Fourteenth Amendment rights.

The Civil Rights Act of 1964 is a pivotal document that affects the rights of many, but especially teachers. The employment of teachers under the *privilege doctrine* was no longer appropriate. Teachers were now entitled to *limited* constitutional rights in their places of work—public schools.

Disputes between teachers and their school boards still arise concerning the actions of teachers both on and off school property. Numerous court cases have been decided not only *for* teachers, but also *against* them.

Balance Out

In the area of freedom of speech or expression *on school grounds*, schools use the Tinker Test for teacher non-curricular speech. The Tinker Test qualifies a teacher's speech as protected as long as it doesn't *materially or substantially disrupt the educational process or invade the rights of others within the school community*.

Can you as a teacher wear an armband or button to protest or promote a cause? What about distributing non-school-sponsored literature on your planning time or using the school's internet mail boxes or school mail routing system to advertise a religious rally? Should you schedule a speaker for your class that is highly controversial or is a religious speaker?

Your religion of choice may be one that requires that you do not recite the Pledge of Allegiance. The school includes the Pledge in its morning activities. Do you refuse to participate? This list of questions can go on and on. Always remind yourself of the Tinker Test. If there is even the slightest doubt, check with the authorities of the school *prior* to engaging in an activity on school property or refusing to participate in a school-sponsored event.

Zero In

Teacher non-school-sponsored speech that occurs *off* school grounds *may* also be scrutinized or be objected to by a school district. Courts do recognize that teachers have the right as citizens to express their views on public matters. However, as courts recognize the need to try to balance the interests of teachers as citizens, they also recognize the need of schools to try to maintain an orderly educational process. Schools *may* attempt to prove that a teacher's speech—even if off school property—*undermined public support* for school officials and school policies or *damaged working conditions* within the school. A public school teacher's right to freedom of speech and/or expression is not unlimited.

If a teacher feels that he or she has been reprimanded, demoted, transferred, or dismissed for a violation of his or her free speech rights, whether in or out of school, here are the questions the courts want answered:

- Did the teacher's speech address a matter of public concern?
- Was the actual or potential disruptive effect of the speech enough to warrant disciplining the teacher?

If the *teacher* can prove that their speech is *protected speech* and that the *protected speech* was a substantial factor in the school board's decision to discipline him or her, then the decision to discipline the teacher may be reversed. *Protected speech* must address a matter of public concern and must not substantially undermine the school district's goals. Following are two examples.

In *Pickering v. Board of Education of Township High School District 205*, 391 U.S. 563, 88 S.Ct. 1731 (1968), the court upheld the rights of this teacher's freedom of expression. The teacher, Mr. Pickering, wrote a letter to the local newspaper criticizing the school superintendent and the school board for spending school funds on athletics and neglecting to inform the taxpayers of this decision. The school board terminated Mr. Pickering's employment for writing this letter.

The court determined that Mr. Pickering's letter did *not* disrupt the school's orderly educational process nor did it defame the character of either the superintendent or the school board because the statements were true. His letter *was* protected speech. His letter addressed facts related to public concern and did not disrupt the school process. Thus, Mr. Pickering was reinstated and returned to his teaching position.

A second case *Mount Healthy City School District Board of Education v. Doyle*, 429 U.S. 274, 97 S.Ct. 568 (1977), again addressed the issue of a teacher's freedom of speech rights. Mr. Doyle, the teacher, had exhibited the following behaviors in and out of school. At school, Mr. Doyle made obscene gestures to female students, swore at students, and participated in several altercations with other employees. Out-of-school speech that Mr. Doyle initiated was a telephone call to a local radio station divulging a memo that the school principal had circulated to several teachers regarding teacher dress and appearance. The radio station announced this memo as an adoption of a dress code for teachers, and it became a news item.

The school board informed Mr. Doyle that he would not be rehired and cited the phone call to the radio station, the making of obscene gestures, and his *lack of tact* in handling professional matters.

The U.S. Supreme Court originally decided in favor of Mr. Doyle. His call to the radio station was *protected speech* and the court ruled that Mr. Doyle be reinstated and receive compensatory damages. His call to the radio station was a matter of public concern.

The court then reversed its decision stating that the school district must be given the opportunity to demonstrate that it would have made the same decision not to rehire Mr. Doyle even without the call to the radio station. This case was remanded back to the Ohio District Court, and indeed the school board proved it would have not rehired Mr. Doyle even if the phone call had not occurred. Ultimately, Mr. Doyle lost his teaching position—if the phone call had been the only incident involving Mr. Doyle, that phone call was *protected speech* (matter of public concern) and Mr. Doyle would have maintained his teaching position.

Remember that the Fourth Amendment of the Constitution (1791) guarantees citizens the "right to be secure in their persons, house, papers, and effects against unreasonable searches and seizures, and no warrant shall be issued, but upon probable cause." This right does extend to public school teachers, but is limited in scope, just as the rights of students to be free from unreasonable searches are limited at school-sponsored events.

Courts have concluded that government employers (school officials) may use the same *reasonable* standard that applies to students also with teachers. In addition, the court rulings have emphasized that public school officials have a direct and overriding interest in ensuring that work of the school is conducted in a proper and efficient manner. Thus, the searches of such facilities as teachers' desks, file cabinets, school owned computers, and offices may be justified if school officials can cite *reasonable causes*.

Maintaining a safe, orderly environment conducive to learning is heavily weighed against both a teacher's and a student's right to privacy. The seriousness of the teacher's "alleged" misconduct may also come into play.

An on going debate still rages on the legality of drug testing of teachers. Teachers' drug testing programs have been challenged in the courts. A

urinalysis test is considered a search and seizure.
School officials must have "reasonable suspicion" to
believe that a teacher may be using an illegal drug,
otherwise the search is impermissible under the Fourth
Amendment. Teachers (or other employees) who are
transporting students are more apt to be tested for
drugs. The safety factor needed when transporting
students many times outweighs the privacy issue of the
employee.

As we have seen, the Gun Free School Zones Act of
1996 prohibits *students* from bringing weapons on
school property. Can teachers whether they have a
license to carry a gun or not--carry a concealed
weapon into a school or onto the school grounds?

State to state, concealed weapons laws vary. Some
states enforce that guns may not be taken into schools
by an adult without the permission of the school
official in charge, and even then guns should be held in
storage. Checking with school authorities for the most
current policy or statute before acting in *any* situation
(unless it's an emergency or crisis) is always

best.

Public school teachers who wish to wear religious garb or to practice their religion on school property may create a problematic situation concerning their First Amendment right to freedom of religion. In addition, Title VII of the Civil Rights Act of 1964 provides even more religious accommodations. Within Title VII, the statute provides that all aspects of religious observances and practices, if requested, must be *assisted* in the workplace. Usually these requests are reasonable and can be accommodated within the school environment. However, if an *employer* can demonstrate that this request *will place an undue hardship on the employer's* business then he or she does not have to accommodate a prospective or current employee's religious request.

Due to the cultural diversity of our country, most school districts have researched these areas thoroughly and should have a policy in place to address a teacher's request for "reasonable" freedom of religious expression in the school setting. Leaves for religious holidays and other expressions of religious activities should be referred to the school district's personnel department. Many items may already be spelled out in the district's master contract. This is another reason why the master contract is a **must** read.

The quest for equality of opportunity in education falls under the equal protection clause of the Fourteenth Amendment. This amendment cites "nor shall any state *deny* to any person within its jurisdiction the equal protection of the laws."

Time and time again, the U.S. Supreme Court has been asked to define and interpret "equal protection of the law." Generically, the Supreme Court has declared that to deny equal protection means to treat a person or a group of persons differently from others *without* a substantial reason.

Previously mentioned in regard to the rights of students, the Civil Rights Act of 1964 began to level the playing field not only for students, but also for school employees. This act barred discrimination in *employment* on the basis of race, gender and religion to any agency or program that receives *any* federal funding. Remember that almost *all* public schools receive some type of federal funding. If a public school was found to have discriminated in any of the above areas, it could lose its federal funding.

The Civil Rights Act of 1991 expanded the Civil Rights Act of 1964. It forbids discrimination in public and/or private employment on the basis of race, gender, color, religion or national origin. A few of the additional topics that are considered within this act are: affirmative action, equal pay, sexual or racial harassment, and hostile environment harassment.

In addition, the Civil Rights Act of 1991 has strengthened both Title VII and Title IX. The independent federal agency charged with prohibiting discrimination in the workplace is the Equal Employment Opportunity Commission (EEOC). Formed in 1965, the EEOC scrutinizes discrimination complaints based on an individual's race, color, national origin, religion, sex, age, or disability. If an employee receives any retaliation for reporting and/or opposing a discriminatory practice in the workplace, the EEOC may also investigate. If the EEOC fails to act or chooses not to take legal action, then the *employee* may go to court with a private suit. By claiming that it is an EEOC employer, the school district should comply with the mandates of this act, and an EEOC office within the school district should monitor any incidents that arise. A few examples of school-related EEOC issues could be: equal pay for coaches, job posting requirements, pregnancy discrimination, family and medical leaves, and sexual harassment to name just a few.

Four other statutes that provide protection for employees are the Rehabilitation Act of 1973, the Age Discrimination in Employment Act of 1978, the American with Disabilities Act of 1990, and the ADA Amendments Act of 2008. Teachers having questions that fall within any of these legal frameworks again should speak to a member of the personnel department in your school district.

Most school districts have policies in place to

handle questions or complaints. They also usually have forms available to lodge complaints for alleged discrimination or mistreatment in all of the areas listed above. Many school districts apply this procedure not only to students, but also to parents, employees, applicants to a school district, or the public in general.

Personnel Issues

Awareness Alert

Local school boards have the authority to assign, reassign, or transfer teachers to specific teaching positions, but their authority can be limited. Limitations of this unilateral control should be defined in the school district's master contract.

Your teaching license is usually the key component in your placement to a teacher position. For example, if your license lists certifications in grades 7-12 science, K-12 special education and music, the school district's administrators can legally place you in any of these teaching areas. Years of experience within a school district (seniority) could play a part in the decision. Also, specific teacher rights listed in the current master contract should be reviewed in the case of a reduction in force situation.

Balance Out

If litigation ensues over an assignment, courts *usually* find in favor of a local school board, if they can prove that through this placement the "rights of students to a thorough and adequate education" have been reached. Your local school district may also be able to *assign* teachers to extracurricular activities. Again, the master contract should be the reference in which the rights of teachers will be documented.

Zero In

First-year teachers, with no experience, usually have to fulfill a probationary period of teaching. Each state varies on what time frame it uses. It can range from 90 school days to two through five school years.

Most states use a tier leveling process by which a teacher can achieve tenure status. The *dismissal* of a teacher can occur at any level of a teacher's career. Even a teacher who has been granted tenure can still be dismissed or have his or her contract terminated.

Most states separate teachers into at least two categories. They are non-permanent and permanent. Categories in some states may include a semi-permanent status as well.

A beginning or non-permanent teacher's contract may be discontinued or not renewed by a local school board for a *less* cause than a permanent teacher. Some school districts need very little *if any* reason to not renew a non-permanent contract. The state in which you are teaching may not even be required to offer to you a due process hearing at this level. Broad reasons that a school district may give for not renewing a non-permanent contract is (1) it is relevant to the best interest of the school district or (2) this teacher was unable to perform his or her teaching duties.

As a permanent status teacher (or even semi-permanent in some states), the reasons to dismiss a teacher become more stringent. Not renewing a contract is the same as a dismissal at this level. Specifically, the teachers who have earned a status of tenure are now entitled to a *property* right to their employment and must be granted *procedural due process* under the Fourteenth Amendment.

Causes for dismissal at this level may also be broadly phrased. Many times courts are brought in to resolve the disputes that arise from these "causes or grounds" used for dismissal. The causes for dismissal usually approved by a state are (but are not limited to): immorality, insubordination, neglect of duty, substantial inability to perform teaching duties (incompetence), good and just cause, and a justifiable decrease in the number of teaching positions (reduction in force).

The case for the dismissal of a teacher's contract may include the following components:

- Documented observations and evaluations of the teacher according to the approved teacher evaluation policy and timelines.
- Proof that formal steps of remediation were undertaken and failed.
- Establishment of a pattern of offending behavior.
- Establishment of a relationship

between the offending behavior and the teacher's effectiveness in the classroom.

- Evidences of prior notices and warnings to the teacher.
- Proof that the teacher's behavior undermined the educational goals of the school.
- Proof of a violation of a written school rule or policy.
- Evidence of incompetence or other similar grounds for dismissal, with evidence based on evaluations by multiple school officials.

Teachers should have *two* personnel files. At the building level, a file is maintained by the principal or the assistant principal in charge of teacher evaluations. Copies of all observations such as evaluations, official reprimands and letters of commendation will be in this file. An identical file should be housed at the school district's central office.

There should *not be one piece of paper in either of these files* that you, as a teacher, have not signed, dated, and been given a copy. If you want to dispute a document, you usually have the right to write a rebuttal statement and have it attached to the original document. Refusing to sign a document that you disagree with *may* be allowable. If you refuse to sign a document, a witness should be called in to verify that you did review the document and refused to sign. The witness will sign the document stating your refusal to sign, and should include the time and date.

It is imperative that you review both the building level file and the central office file every year. If you feel uncomfortable asking to view these files, take a fellow teacher with you or ask a union representative for assistance. Administrators may keep personal notes—these are not available for your review. But again, *nothing* should be in a **teacher's permanent files** that the teacher hasn't seen. Sometimes a document may be removed or purged from a teacher's permanent file after a specified time period. This may be allowed for example, if the infraction or situation has not occurred again. Know your rights.

Key Vocabulary

Protected Speech
Drug Testing
Gun Free School Zones Act of 1996
Title VII of the Civil Rights Act of 1964
Civil Rights Act of 1991
Equal Employment Opportunity Commission
Rehabilitation Act of 1973
Age Discrimination in Employment Act 1978
Americans with Disabilities Act 1990
Probationary Period—Teacher Dismissal
Non-Permanent Teacher Status
Semi-Permanent Teacher Status
Permanent Teacher Status
Due Process Hearings

Notes

Chapter 6: Who Controls What and How You Teach?

Understanding Public School Curriculum

Awareness Alert

What is the basic definition of the <u>curriculum</u> of a public school? Most think that curriculum is a list of required subjects or courses, but it is much broader than just courses of study or textbooks. Curriculums also include the use of *any* supplemental materials such as computers and media, a school's pedagogical practices (such as ability grouping or tracking), and even a classroom teacher's *method* of teaching.

There is a perceived potential that through their curriculums, schools can promote cultural, political, ideological, and even religious beliefs and behaviors. Thus, major educational conflicts and debates have occurred from clashes with parents, teachers, school authorities, and interest groups over the curriculum used in a school.

Balance Out

Since education is the responsibility of the states, control of the curriculum is shared by state legislatures, state departments of education and their state school boards, and local school boards. Minimum standards of achievement and policies requiring specific courses for public school students are usually set at the state level. Most states then give local school boards the authority to regulate instructional programs and to approve of the curriculum.

Zero In

Individual teachers may conclude that they have the right to "academic freedom" since the U. S. Supreme Court has yet to define academic freedom at the elementary or secondary levels. However, states, local school districts, and teachers do not have the complete authority to offer or require any or all curriculums without question. If an instructional complaint is lodged, and it can be framed as a violation of the constitution, a lawsuit may be filed.

Dealing With Objections to Programs or Content

Awareness Alert

The First Amendment of the Constitution (passed in 1791) states that "Congress shall make no law respecting an establishment of religion, or prohibiting the free exercise there of: or, abridging the freedom of speech, or of the press; or the right of the people peaceably to assemble." Many of the topics addressed in the First Amendment still cause controversy.

The principle in the First Amendment that refers to religion has been interpreted by the courts to mean a *wall of separation between church and state.* Since schools are an arm and the responsibility of the state, many religious activities within schools have been questioned. For example posting the Ten Commandments, instruction in creation and/or evolution, and the study of religious materials in schools all continues to raise objections and spark disputes.

Public schools and their staffs may curb religious challenges if they take a *neutral* approach to religion. The role of educators is not to either *promote* or *inhibit* the free exercise of religion. Your administrators should know how to **balance** the religious rights of all based on the recent decisions of the courts. Ask, if you are unsure.

Balance Out

Guaranteeing freedom of speech or of the press is also a right listed in the First Amendment. Debates over the appropriateness of programs such as sex education, character or moral development, and AIDS information (to name a few) have been numerous and on going. In addition, requiring the recitation of the Pledge of Allegiance for students in public schools has been tested since 1943 (*West Virginia State Board of Education v. Barnett*, 319 U.S. 624 (1943).
Supplemental materials, library books, media

materials, and even school theatrical productions have also been criticized using these same arguments.

Zero In

The courts seem to agree that the use of materials that can be determined to be obscene, vulgar, or sexually offensive *may* be removed from schools. The dilemma for educators in these situations is that the courts did not define the terms listed above. Also, if the material in question can be judged as racially, sexually, gender or ethnically biased, it may also be discarded.   The obligation to provide an unbiased and sound curriculum rests with the local education authorities, including the local school board, and ultimately with you, the individual teacher. Always consider:

> *the age and grade level of the students
> *the relevancy of the questioned material to the
>   approved curriculum
> *the length of time the materials are to be used
> *the general acceptance of a disputed teaching
>   method within the profession such as visioning
> *prior existence of board policy* governing

selection of materials and teaching techniques.

Request copies of your local school board's policies on: copyright compliance, fair use, censorship, computer use, and internet use for students and employees.

Key Vocabulary

Public School Curriculum
Academic Freedom for PreK-12 Teachers
Obscene, Vulgar or Sexually Offensive Materials
Copyright Compliance
Fair Use Policy for Materials, Media, and Internet
Censorship Policies
Computer/Internet Usage Polices for Student & Staff

Notes

Chapter 7: How Do I Treat Every Student Equally and Differently at the Same Time?

Students with Special Needs

Awareness Alert

Before the 1970s, most children with disabilities *could not* or *did not* attend public schools. Section 504 of the 1973 the Rehabilitation Act was passed by Congress in 1977. This act required that "no otherwise qualified individual with handicaps shall solely by reason of his or her handicap, be excluded from participation in, denied the benefits of, or be subjected to discrimination under any program or activity receiving federal funds."

The Education for All Handicapped Children Act was passed in 1975 and has transformed over the years into the Individuals with Disabilities Education Act (IDEA, 1997). The Section 504 plan grew out of the Civil Rights Act of 1964 and requires special accommodations for any student with a qualifying condition. IDEA was reauthorized and rewritten in 2004 (Siegel, 2009). Along with Section 504, IDEA, the American with Disabilities Act of 1990 (ADA), and the ADA Amendments Act of 2008, the disabled and their rights are protected in this country.

Balance Out

Basically, there are two main avenues that teachers or parents can pursue to determine if a child may have a disability and may qualify for assistance. These procedures are available through both *Section 504* and *IDEA*.

Section 504 of the Rehabilitation Act of 1973 was enacted to eliminate discrimination on the basis of disabilities in any program or activity receiving federal funds. This act protects not just disabled students but *any person* (there are no age restrictions) "who has a physical or mental impairment which *substantially limits* one or more of such person's major life activities, has a *record* of such impairment, or is regarded as having such impairment." Major life activities include caring for oneself, performing manual tasks, walking, seeing, hearing, speaking, breathing, learning, and working.

IDEA (formerly called P.L. 94-142) requires *public schools* to make available to all eligible children (ages three through 22 years—these ages may vary from state to state) with disabilities *a free appropriate* public education in the *least restrictive environment* appropriate to their individual needs (National Center for Children and Youth with Disabilities, 1997).

Zero In

First and foremost, remember that even though Section 504 and IDEA parallel each other, there are *key* differences. The most important contrast is that Section 504 *does not receive* any federal funding, but IDEA *does*. For the student that is eligible under Section 504, *the local school district must pay* for expenses incurred by implementing the Section 504 plan.

Federal funding is provided to help states with the cost of special education under IDEA.

Second, even though there is no funding for eligible students under Section 504, **both** federal statutes **are** mandates. This means that if a student has *either* a special education file known as an individualized education program (IEP) or a Section 504 alternative learning plan (ALP), teachers **must** comply with the provisions in these documents. *All students eligible under IDEA are also eligible for Section 504.* However, the reverse is not true. *All students eligible under Section 504 may or may not be eligible for IDEA.* Some disabilities such as attention deficient disorders or attention deficient hyper disorders qualify for services under Section 504, but not under IDEA. This is because each state may interpret Section 504 and IDEA differently.

Individual school districts must maintain compliance with Section 504. *How* each school district chooses to comply with this federal mandate is completely at the discretion of the school district.

Each school district is responsible for interpreting, implementing, and documenting its own Section 504 procedures. Some approaches school districts may take are:

- appoint a district-wide Section 504 coordinator.
- develop and implement a Section 504 compliance plan.
- communicate the compliance plan to the public. Ensure that referral forms are available.
- convene a Section 504 conference committee to evaluate and issue a report.
- develop an Alternate Learning Plan (ALP) if a student is eligible for a Section 504 plan.
- encourage parent participation and permission which are highly recommended but not required.
- suggest related services that will not be funded.
- re-evaluate the student: this is required— *when* this will occur should be established in the ALP.

To receive federal funding from IDEA, all states must develop a plan for providing for the disabled children within their state. This plan must be a free and appropriate public education program, which emphasizes special education with related services designed to meet the unique needs of disabled students. In addition, this plan includes a system to allocate the federal funds to local school districts. Then, each school district must submit its plan to the state indicating how it will, as a local school district, comply with the IDEA requirements. There is not much latitude with most of the requirements; most are very straightforward.

However, the scope of the "least restrictive environment" for each school district is one that may vary. Actual classroom placement philosophies can range from mainstreaming the student to offering full inclusion programs. The phrase "least restrictive environment" is very easy to misinterpret. It is imperative, as a new teacher, that you know which "least restrictive environment" plan exists in your school district.

IDEA mandates that public school systems adhere to the following requirements:

- request for a diagnostic and/or psychological referral made by an administrator, teacher(s), parent(s) or legal guardian

- parent/legal guardian interview—notice of referral, rights and parental/legal guardian permission to evaluate

- multidisciplinary educational evaluation

- convene a case conference committee

- case conference committee to approve eligibility for special education placement

- write an Individualized Education Program (IEP)

- provide and fund related services if needed

- review the IEP: required annually by IEP Committee

- require re-evaluation every three years if student still receives special education services.

The uses of procedural safeguards are fundamental when disciplining a special needs student. A special needs student can certainly be disciplined, but certain disciplines can trigger many additional requirements under IDEA. Educators, who are members of the IEP Committee, special education teachers, or administrators, will be able to provide you with a definition and a working knowledge of: behavioral intervention plans, functional behavioral assessments, manifestation determinations, change of placement requirements, and the stay-put rule. Following the most current reauthorizations of IDEA and Section 504 is critical. Legislation can change on a yearly basis. Meeting the needs of a special education student is very challenging, complex, and cannot ever be ignored.

Key Vocabulary

Section 504--1973
Education for All Handicapped Children Act, 1975
P.L. 94-142
Individual with Disabilities Education Act (IDEA), 1997
Free Appropriate Public Education (FAPE)
Least Restrictive Environment
Alternative Learning Plan (ALP)
Individualized Education Program (IEP)

Notes

Chapter 8: What Happens if I Am Sued?

Understanding Torts & Liability

Awareness Alert

Unfortunately today, the "American way" to solve disputes is to sue. *Tort law* provides this "way" for parents and guardians to sue the school district for wrongful harm to one's (usually the child's) body, property, or reputation.

A typical tort lawsuit involves a parent suing a school for an injury that occurs at school or during a school-sponsored activity. Tort suits usually *name everyone that could be related to the accident*. This may include the teacher(s), school nurse, guidance counselor, possibly the secretary, the custodian, and always the principal. Many times the school board and the school district are listed as defendants as well, because it is the school district that provides the liability insurance coverage for its employees while they are working on school time.

If you are *not* "on the clock" at school or at a school-sponsored activity—you could get sued *personally.* Make sure that if you drive a vehicle for the school district that you have the proper license and are cleared and covered by the school district's insurance. Do *not* put students in your personal vehicles and transport them if you have *not* been granted permission by the school board to do so.

The usual remedy sought by parents is monetary damage. If an activity is ruled by the courts to be dangerous or extremely hazardous, then courts may issue an injunction to prohibit the continuation of the harmful activity.

Practicing the suggestions outlined in this chapter *will not protect* you, entirely from being sued, but it will provide an overview of tort law for beginning teachers that should assist you if you are ever named in a law suit. The most important rule of thumb is to **stop and think** before you act or make a decision.

Balance Out

Failure is a word that most folks, and especially schools, dislike—even more so in the area of tort liability lawsuits. In the tort liability lawsuit area, *negligence* can be defined as *the failure to exercise reasonable care.* All too often, this failure to exercise reasonable care results in harm to another person.

If harm does occur to a student, and a tort liability lawsuit is filed, the court system reviews four elements to determine whether or not there may be a finding of negligence:

1. duty and standard of care
2. breach of duty
3. proximate cause
4. injury with the awarding of damages.

Zero In

Can you prevent an accident from occurring? Maybe you can, but maybe you can't. Safety *must* be the cornerstone of all schools. Parents can and will file lawsuits even when teachers, principals, and schools do everything right. Unfortunately, teachers can't stop parents from suing, but *you* can be proactive, knowledgeable of tort law and know and follow your school district's policies.

As an educator, you have a *legal duty* to students to provide a high standard of care. Teachers, principals, and most other school employees are held to this higher standard of behavior, because students are 'under the school's care" during the school day and at school-sponsored activities.

Accidents will always happen. Especially when kids are present. No one is liable for accidents that are *unavoidable, not foreseeable, or not preventable* with reasonable and prudent precautions. However, if we *fail* to live up to this duty and high standard of care and an accident, injury or harm to another person does occur, there may be grounds for liability and negligence.

The *key* to establish a breach of legal duty is to

determine whether a teacher's conduct fell *below* the required *high* standard of care expected of all teachers. Should the teacher have *foreseen* the resulting injury? If the answers are **yes,** then a breach of duty will probably be found. By knowing your school's policy regarding supervision, safety precautions, and crisis plans, you may avoid a legally dangerous situation. If the *school's own policy* was violated then a breach of duty is more likely to be found.

Understanding and following your school district's policies could make the difference in whether a court can establish a breach of duty. Remember though, many times parents can and will sue even if the policies are followed.

Parents (and their attorneys) who sue and file tort liability lawsuits believe that not only a breach of duty occurred but also that a proximate cause exists. In other words, did the *act* cause the injury? Or was the act sufficiently connected to the injury to be considered its cause? Two examples:

- Students were working on an experiment in

science lab. A 250-watt light bulb and two containers of water and sand with thermometers in them were being used. Students were arranged on both sides of the bulb. One student flicked water onto the hot glass bulb and it exploded. Glass struck several students in the eyes. No goggles were being worn. The *act* of the teacher to not require students to wear goggles during this experiment was definitely a cause of the eye injury. This teacher should have *foreseen* that the lack of wearing safety eyewear could result in harm.

- An art teacher sent a student to a chemistry stockroom to obtain concentrated nitric acid for an etching project. The student accidentally spilled the nitric acid on herself and burned her arm. Proper first aid was administered and the student was rushed to the emergency room of the nearest hospital. The *act* of the art teacher sending a *student* to obtain a chemical from the chemical storeroom (which should have been locked in the first place) was directly connected to the injury this student suffered. This teacher (or another adult such as an aide or custodian) should have retrieved the chemical. The teacher should have thought this action through more carefully.

If the tort suit case makes it to a court of law and the court finds a breach of duty and proximate cause, the most common award is *compensatory damages*. The purpose of this is to compensate the injured persons for their actual losses. Many tort lawsuits today not only include reimbursement for medical expenses, but also compensation for lost salary of parents, court costs, and legal fees. In addition, courts are now awarding expenses for psychological injury and/or emotional distress.

Remember to always err on the side of safety. For example, two elementary students on the way to school find some blasting caps at a construction site *(Miller v. Griesel*, 308 N.E. 2d 701, 704-05 (Ind. 1974). When the teacher leaves the room, the students accidentally set off the caps and an explosion occurs. There was no way that the teacher could have foreseen this accident.

Sometimes a student's (or other students) own negligence can contribute to and/or cause the injury. In these situations, courts may consider the student guilty of *contributory* negligence. In the case mentioned above, the court found that the teacher and the school were *not* liable. In a contributory negligence situation, courts do consider the age and maturity of the student to determine the ruling. However, courts also will still investigate *what was done prior, by the teacher and the school, to prevent such an injury.*

If an accident does occur, first provide the proper first aid and medical attention, and then notify the school authorities. As soon as possible after the accident, document the incident by listing the details prior, during, and after the incident including date, time and response time. If this unfortunate situation becomes the basis for a tort liability lawsuit, you may be required to participate in a legal deposition, and this documentation will be helpful.

Ask your school crisis/safety team to review the incident and examine what the school and all teachers can learn from this situation. The principal should update faculty and staff with these findings and review safety procedures for the school in general.

Occasionally, tort lawsuits may be settled *out of court* by the school district's insurance company in conjunction with the parents, along with their attorneys. Due to the high cost of legal fees and the time involved in a tort lawsuit, an insurance company may issue a one-time compensatory damage award. If this occurs, accept the decision, even though you *may not* believe that you violated your duty or high standard of care.

Teachers who understand the school district's policies regarding supervision, and who not only model but practice excellent safety precautions, enhance the educational experience for *all* of their students.

Key Vocabulary

Tort Law
Liability
Negligence
Duty and Standard of Care
Breach of Duty
Proximate Cause
Injury and Awarding of Damages
Foreseeable
Compensatory Damages
Contributory Negligence

Notes

Chapter 9: Summary

Always Do What Is Best for Kids

Education is complex, challenging, and ever-changing. As a teacher, you have the opportunity every day to affect not only the knowledge base of your students, but also to affect their lives. A career in teaching is much more than improving student achievement. It is first and foremost all about people.

The law, especially pertaining to schools, can change rapidly. Federal statutes may be amended annually. State statutes can change each time a state holds a legislative session. For example, this past month (March, 2010), in the state of Florida, a bill requiring teacher pay to be tied to the performance of students was passed. Two other bills in Florida await passage that will also greatly impact teachers as well. One such bill states that rather than basing a teacher's retirement pay on the average of the five highest years of pay during a teacher's career, the retirement pay will be based on an average of the teacher's pay during their entire career—from the first year to the last. Florida legislatures are also trying to remove any semi-permanent or permanent status (tenure) for teachers. This state is pushing for a one year contract annually—the teacher may or may not be relieved of their duties after one year of service with no due process hearing.

This author believes that ultimately teachers will have to carry malpractice insurance. If a teacher's pay is tied to student performance and parents do not perceive that their child reached a specified achievement level, parents may begin to file academic malpractice suits. In this author's opinion, a formula should be developed to weight the child's cognitive index score (IQ) with other factors relating to the economic factors of the school and the level of parental support received.

After reading this book, many legal questions have been raised. Hopefully, the unanswered questions will encourage you to dig deeper into the topic of school law or at least the minimum to know and understand your local school district's policies. Two parting suggestions: (1) always be an **ethical** and **honest** teacher and (2) always do what is **best** for kids.

Appendix A

The Constitution of the United States of America

[Sections of the Constitution that pertain to school law]

Preamble

We the People of the United States, in Order to form a more perfect Union, establish Justice, insure domestic Tranquility, provide for the common defense, promote the general Welfare, and secure the Blessings of Liberty to ourselves and our Posterity, do ordain and establish this Constitution for the United States of America.

Amendment I (1791)

Congress shall make no law respecting an establishment of religion, or prohibiting the free exercise thereof; or abridging the freedom of speech, or the press; or the right of the people peaceably to assemble, and to petition the Government for a redress of grievances.

Amendment IV (1791)

The right of the people to be secure in their persons, houses, papers, and effects, against unreasonable searches and seizures, shall not be violated, and no Warrants shall issue, but upon probable cause, supported by Oath or affirmation, and particularly describing the place to be searched, and the persons or things to be seized.

Amendment V (1791)

No person shall be held to answer for a capital, or otherwise infamous crime, unless on a presentment or indictment of a Grand Jury, except in cases arising in the land or naval forces, or in the Militia, when in actual service in time of Was or public danger; nor shall any person be subject for the same offence to be twice put in jeopardy of life or limb; nor shall be compelled in any criminal case to be a witness against himself, nor be deprived of life, liberty, or property without due process of law; nor shall private property be taken for public use, without just compensation.

Amendment VI (1791)

In all criminal prosecutions, the accused shall enjoy the right to a speedy and public trial, by an impartial jury of the State and district wherein the crime shall have been committed, which district shall have bee previously ascertained by law, and to be informed of the nature and the cause of the accusation; to be confronted with the witnesses against him; to have compulsory process for obtaining Witnesses in his favor, and to have the Assistance of Counsel for his defense.

Amendment VII (1791)

In suits of common law, where the value in controversy shall exceed twenty dollars, the right of trial by jury shall be preserved, and no fact tried by a jury, shall be otherwise re-examined in any Court of the United States, than according to the rules of common law.

Amendment VIII (1791)

Excessive bail shall not be required, nor excessive fines imposed, nor cruel and unusual punishments inflicted.

Amendment IX (1791)

The enumeration in the Constitution, of certain rights, shall not be construed to deny or disparage others retained by the people.

Amendment X (1791)

The powers not delegated to the United States by the Constitution, nor prohibited by it to the States, are reserved to the States respectively, or to the people.

Amendment XI (1798)

The Judicial power of the United States shall not be construed to extend to any suit in law or equity, commenced or prosecuted against one of the United States by Citizens of another State, or by Citizens or

Subjects of any Foreign State.

Amendment XIV (1868)

Section 1. All persons born or naturalized in the United States and subject to the jurisdiction there of, are citizens of the United States and of the State wherein they reside. No state shall make or enforce any law which shall abridge the privileges or immunities of citizens of the United States; nor shall any State deprive any person of life, liberty, or property, without due process of law; nor deny to any person within its jurisdiction the equal protection of the laws.

Amendment XV (1870)

Section 1. The right of citizens of the United States to vote shall not be denied or abridged by the United States or by any State on account of race, color, or previous condition of servitude.

Section 2. The congress shall have power to enforce this article by appropriate legislation.

Amendment XIX (1920)

Section 1. The rights of the citizens of the United States to vote shall not be denied or abridged by the United States or by any State on account of sex.

Section 2. Congress shall have the power to enforce this article by appropriate legislation.

Amendment XXVI (1971)

Section 1. The right of citizens of the United State, who are eighteen years of age or older, to vote shall not be denied or abridged by the United States or by any State on account of age.

Section 2. The Congress shall have the power to enforce this article by appropriate legislation.

Appendix B

Court Cases Cited

Bagget v. Bullitt, 377 U.S. 360 (1964)

Bethel School District No. 403 v. Fraser, 478 U.S. 675 (1986)

Brown v. Board of Education, 347 U.S. 483 (1954)

Cole v. Oroville Union Highs School, 229 F.3d 1092 (9th Cir. 2000)

Gonzaga University v. Doe, 536 U.S. 273 (2002)

Hazelwood School District v. Kuhlmeier, 484 U.S. 260 (1988)

Keyishian v. Board of Regents 385 U.S. 589 (1967)

Miller v. Griesel, 308 N.E. 2d 701, 704-05 (Ind. 1974)

Mount Healthy City School District Board of Education v. Doyle, 429 U.S. 274, 97 S.Ct. 568 (1977)

Pickering v. Board of Education of Township High School District 205, 391 U.S. 563, 88 S.Ct. 1731 (1968)

Plyler v. Doe, 457 U.S. 202 (1982)

Settle v. Dickson County School Board, 53 F.3d 152 (6th Cir. 1995)

Tinker v. Des Moines Independent Community School District, 393 U.S. 503 (1969)

West Virginia State Board of Education v. Barnett, 319 U.S. 624 (1943)

Appendix C

References

AFL/CIO, Public Employee Department. (1997). Public Employees Bargain for Excellence. Washington DC: AFL-CIO.

Center for Education Reform. (2009). Charter School Laws Across the States. htpp://www.edreform.com/About_CER/Charter School_Laws_Across_the_States/index.cfm.

Clark, S. G. (2001). Confidentiality and disclosure: A lesson in sharing. Principal Leadership, 1(8), 40-43.

Eskenazi, S. (1999). Learning Curves. Houston Press. http://www.houstonpress.com/1999-07-22/news/learning-curves/2.

Essex, N. L. (2001). The limits of zero tolerance. Principal Leadership, 1(8), 5-7.

Haynes, C. C., Chaltan, S., Ferguson, J., Hudson, D., & Thomas, O. (2003). The First Amendment in the Schools. Alexandria, VA: Association for Supervision and Curriculum Development.

Indiana Department of Education. (1999) . Checklist for a Safe and Secure School Environment, Indianapolis, IN: Marian College.

Imber, M.., & van Geel, T. (1995) . A Teacher's Guide to Education Law. New York: McGraw-Hill, Inc.

Jehen, A. (2008, October). Overdose? NeaTODAY Magazine. pp. 33.

Kelly, E. B. (2006) . Legal Basics—A Handbook for Educators. Bloomington, In: Phi Delta Kappa International.

Kyler, R. (2007) . To the state they are A students; to the fed, they're left behind. Northwest Florida Daily News, Feb. 25. A1, A10.

Mawdsley, R. D. (2001) . Let us pray? Principal Leadership, 1(8), 20-25.

McKinney, J. R., JD., Ed.D. (1992) . Indiana School Law—The Legal Rights and Responsibilities of Indiana Public School Educators. Muncie, Indiana: Ball State University.

Nathan, J. (1996) . Charter Schools: Creating Hope and Opportunity for American Education. San Francisco: Jossey Bass.

National Information Center for Children and Youth with Disabilities. (1997, August). The IDEA Amendments of 1997. Washington, DC: NICHCY News Digest.

O'Neill, S. (2001). A "fine" relationship: OSHA and schools. Principal Leadership, 1(8), 38-39.

Permuth, S. & Mawdsley, R. D. (2001). The supreme court on education: Five defining cases. Principal Leadership, 1(8), 29-33.

Petzko, V. N. (2001). Preventing legal headaches. Principal Leadership, 1(8), 34-37.

Public Service Research Foundation. (1994). State Public Sector Bargaining Statutes. Vienna, Virginia: PSRF.

Rodkin, D. (2009). Charting a new course. Chicago Magazine. 58, 56-63.

Roche, B. A. (2004). Law 101. Naperville, IL: Sphinx Publishing.

Russell, A. (2007). In-state tution for undocumented immigrants: States' rights and educational opportunity. American Association of State Colleges and Universities, aascu.org.

Russo, C. J., & Mawdsley, R. D. (2002). Education Law. New York, NY: Law Journal Press.

Sharkey, N. S. & Murnane, R. J. (2003) . Learning from student assessment results. <u>Educational Leadership</u>, <u>61</u>(3), 77-81.

Sendor, B. (1995) . Be firm, be fair, and pay attention to due process. <u>The American School Board Journal</u>, <u>1</u>, 16-17.

Siegel, L. M. (2009) . <u>The Complete IEP Guide— How to Advocate for Your Special Ed Child.</u> Berkeley, CA: Consolidated Printers, Inc.

Smith, J. (1997). <u>School Crisis Management Manual—Guidelines for Administrators.</u> Holmes Beach, FL: Learning Publications, Inc.

Streshly, W. A., Walsh, J., & Frase, L.E. (2002) . <u>Avoiding Legal Hassles, What School Administrators Really Need to Know.</u> Thousand Oaks, CA: Corwin Press, Inc.

Thomas, E. & Wingert, P. (2010) . Why we must fire bad teachers: In no other profession are workers so insulated from accountability. <u>Newsweek</u>, Mar 15.

Vock, D. C. (2007, December 13) . With Feds Stuck, States take on Immigration. htpp://www.stateline.org/live/printable/story?contentId =264483.

Whitaker, S. (1998). Safe Schools. Indiana University Southeast Educational Leadership Certification Program. New Albany, IN: Indiana University Southeast.

Zuckerbrod, N. (2010, February 13). Illegal Students Await Immigration Plan. USATODAY.com: Gannett Co. Inc.

About the Author

Photograph by Paula Doolin

Dr. McNames received her undergraduate degree in 1972 from the University of Kentucky, Lexington Kentucky. She majored in elementary education and minored in literature. Dr. McNames began her teaching career in the Pittsburg City Schools, Pittsburg, Pennsylvania. After staying in Pittsburgh for three years she spent ten years teaching in the New Albany-Floyd County School Corporation, New Albany, Indiana. In 1978, she received a Masters in Elementary Education and a Guidance and Counseling endorsement from Indiana University Southeast in New Albany, Indiana. She then began work on her Educational Specialist Degree at Indiana University, Bloomington, Indiana. This degree included a principal and superintendent certificate and was completed in 1985.

From 1985-1993 Dr. McNames was a middle school guidance counselor and then an elementary principal. In 1995, she received her doctorate from the University of Louisville in Educational Leadership. From 1994-2003 she served as the Coordinator of the

Educational Leadership Certification Program and was promoted from an assistant professor to an associate professor at Indiana University Southeast, New Albany, Indiana. She was appointed to the State Planning Board for the Indiana Association of Elementary and Secondary Principals in 1989. In addition, Dr. McNames served as a consultant to the Indiana Department of Education from 1990-1995 as on site reviewer for the Performance-Based Accreditation Program.

Dr. McNames has received numerous teaching awards and scholarships: Scottish Rite Foundation Fellow Scholarship, Indiana Principal Leadership Academy Fellow, Outstanding Faculty of Adult Learners Award, the FACET Award—Faculty Colloquium & Excellence in Teaching, and the Gerald Read International Seminar Scholarship from Phi Delta Kappa. In addition, she is the recipient of three TERAs—Teaching Excellence Recognition Awards and two Trustees Teaching Awards—all from Indiana University.

This life-long learner and educator is the founder and the CEO of The Educational Leadership Academy, LLC. The ABZ's of School Law for Teachers is her first book.

Products and Services

To purchase the book

The ABZ's of School Law for Teachers

Contact:

Dr. Patricia McNames
The Educational Leadership Academy, LLC
www.schoollaw101.com
or
pmcnameskunkel@cox.net

Order forms may be sent to
755 Grand Blvd #B 105-309
Miramar Beach, FL 32550

Product	Price	Quantity	Total
The ABZ's of School Law for Teachers	16.95		
Shipping & Handling per book	3.99		